Edge Books

Ragdoll Cats

by Joanne Mattern

CAPSTONE PRESS
a capstone imprint

Edge Books are published by Capstone Press,
151 Good Counsel Drive, P.O. Box 669, Mankato, Minnesota 56002.
www.capstonepub.com

Books published by Capstone Press are manufactured with paper containing at least 10 percent post-consumer waste.

Library of Congress Cataloging-in-Publication Data
Mattern, Joanne, 1963-
Ragdoll cats / by Joanne Mattern.
p. cm.—(Edge books. All about cats)
Includes bibliographical references and index.
Summary: "Describes the history, physical features, and care of the Ragdoll cat breed"—Provided by publisher.
ISBN 978-1-4296-6867-5 (library binding)
1. Ragdoll cat—Juvenile literature. I. Title.
SF449.R34M384 2012
636.8'3—dc22 2011009804

Editorial Credits

Connie R. Colwell and Carrie Braulick Sheely, editors; Gene Bentdahl, designer; Wanda Winch, media researcher; Eric Manske, production specialist

Photo Credits

Alamy: Tierfotogaentur, cover; Photo by Fiona Green, 6, 23, 25, 26, 28; Ragdoll Fanciers Club International, 10, 11; Shutterstock: Linn Currie, 5, 12, 15, 16, 18, 19, 21; SuperStock Inc.: Marka, 9

Printed in the United States of America in Stevens Point, Wisconsin.
112011 006475R

TABLE OF CONTENTS

Chapter 1

CALM COMPANIONS

Many cats are named for their place of origin. Others are named for their physical characteristics. But the Ragdoll gets its name from a behavior. When picked up, some Ragdolls go limp. Picking up a Ragdoll cat resembles picking up a rag doll.

The Ragdoll breed has gained widespread popularity throughout the world. In 2009 the Ragdoll was the fifth most popular breed in the Cat Fanciers' Association (CFA). It was the third most popular longhaired breed. The CFA is the world's largest cat **registry**.

Many people enjoy the unique combination of the Ragdoll's personality and appearance. Ragdolls make a big statement with their large size, **colorpoints**, and silky fur. Yet the cats have understated personalities. Ragdolls are quiet, gentle, and affectionate. The breed's personality makes it popular with people who want a calm companion.

registry—an organization that keeps track of the ancestry for cats of a certain breed

colorpoint—a pattern in which the ears, face, tail, and feet are darker than the base color

FACT: Ragdolls are similar in appearance and personality to Maine Coon cats. Both breeds have earned the nickname "gentle giants."

Some Ragdolls have dark brown colorpoints that stand out well against their light body color.

Ragdolls are calm as adults, but Ragdoll kittens are very playful.

IS THE RAGDOLL RIGHT FOR YOU?

Ragdolls make good family pets. They get along well with dogs and other cats. Ragdolls' easygoing personalities help them fit in with busy families. They don't demand attention as often as some other breeds do.

Ragdolls have few health problems and are generally easy to care for. But because they have long hair, Ragdolls need to be brushed weekly.

FINDING A RAGDOLL

You can find a Ragdoll in several ways. Visiting a breeder is one of the best ways to find a Ragdoll. Responsible breeders carefully select their cats for breeding. They make sure that the cats are healthy.

Adopting a cat is usually much less expensive than buying one from a breeder. You may be able to adopt a Ragdoll through a breed rescue organization or an animal shelter. These organizations help find new, loving homes for pets. Some Ragdolls from breed rescue organizations might even be registered with the CFA or another registry.

Chapter 2

RAGDOLL HISTORY

The Ragdoll is one of the newest cat breeds. It was developed in the 1960s in California.

A POPULAR MYTH

A myth exists about the origin of Ragdolls. This story says that the breed was created after a car accidentally struck a pregnant longhaired white cat. The cat's brain was damaged as a result of the accident. This injury changed the cat's personality. The cat became extremely quiet and gentle. Following the accident, the cat's body also went limp when held. The cat later gave birth to kittens. These kittens were born with the same limp body and gentle personality as their mother.

This story about Ragdolls is not true. A cat's personality and physical condition can change as a result of an accident. But it is impossible for these changes to be passed to the cat's offspring.

Ragdoll kittens often look and act similar to their parents.

Ann Baker holds Fugianna, a female cat that helped develop the Ragdoll breed.

A NEW BREED TAKES OFF

Ann Baker of Riverside, California, developed the Ragdoll breed in the early 1960s. Baker bred a longhaired white cat named Josephine to another longhaired cat. It is believed that these cats had markings similar to those of the Siamese, a breed with colorpoints. The mating produced a **mitted**, **seal-point** male named Daddy Warbucks. This cat had a cream-colored coat with dark points. He also had white markings on all four of his paws.

mitted—a color pattern that includes white foot markings and white markings on the stomach, chin, and chest

seal-point—a colorpoint pattern in which the points are very dark brown

Many people believe Daddy Warbucks and other relatives of Josephine are the breed's foundation cats. It is not known what breeds Baker used to develop the Ragdoll. Some people believe Baker used Persian, Birman, and Burmese cats. Other people don't believe Baker used purebred cats. They think she selected mixed-breed longhaired cats with certain features for her breeding program.

Daddy Warbucks (above) is known for developing the mitted color pattern in the Ragdoll breed.

People can purchase Ragdoll kittens from breeders when the cats are 12 to 16 weeks old.

A NEW BREED IS RECOGNIZED

In 1971 Baker founded the International Ragdoll Cat Association (IRCA). Baker had strict rules about how her Ragdolls should be bred. But cat associations did not recognize IRCA Ragdolls. Owners could not enter these cats in cat shows.

Other breeders did not agree with the IRCA rules. Two of these breeders were Denny and Laura Dayton. The Daytons decided to develop the breed so that other cat associations would accept it.

The Daytons bought a pair of IRCA Ragdolls. Starting with these two cats, they created a standard breeding program for Ragdolls. In 1975 the Daytons and other Ragdoll breeders formed the Ragdoll Fanciers Club International. This club tried to build interest in the breed.

Eventually, the breeders' work paid off. The CFA allowed the Ragdoll to be shown in its miscellaneous class in 1993. In 2000 the CFA officially accepted the Ragdoll.

FACT: Ragdolls have quiet meows. They meow less than many other breeds.

Chapter 3

STRONG AND SILKY

Ragdolls are large cats. They can weigh 20 pounds (9.1 kilograms) or more. Male Ragdolls usually weigh between 14 and 18 pounds (6.4 and 8.2 kg). Females usually weigh between 8 and 12 pounds (3.6 and 5.4 kg). It may take up to four years for Ragdolls to reach their full size.

BODY

Ragdolls have sturdy, long bodies with good **proportion**. Broad legs and large, round paws support the cats' muscular frames. Ragdolls have full, long tails.

COAT

A Ragdoll's fur is long, thick, and soft. Ragdolls have a double coat. A thin layer of plush fur lies near the skin. This undercoat is covered by a layer of lightweight, long, silky fur. The Ragdoll's fur does not easily clump together in mats like the coats of some other longhaired breeds.

proportion—the relation of one part to another; animals have good proportion when one body part doesn't seem too large or too small when compared to another part

FACT: Ragdolls may have tufts of fur between their toes.

The long, thick coat of the Ragdoll adds to its full-bodied appearance.

red-point Ragdoll

Ragdolls often have a **ruff**. The hair on their faces and shoulders is often shorter than it is on the rest of their bodies.

POINT COLORS

All Ragdolls have colorpoints. Ragdoll kittens are born white. The points begin to appear when the kittens are a few days old. Ragdolls' permanent coat color patterns develop by the time they are 4 years old.

ruff—long hairs growing around an animal's neck

Ragdolls that have no color pattern other than points are simply called colorpoints. A colorpoint Ragdoll's coat has no white fur.

Points can be one of several colors. These colors include seal, chocolate, blue, and lilac. Points can also be red, cinnamon, cream, and fawn. Seal is dark brown, and chocolate is light brown. The blue color is blue-gray, and the lilac color is pink-gray. Red-point Ragdolls have red-orange points. On cinnamon-point Ragdolls, the points are red-brown. Cream ranges from dark off-white to very light brown. The fawn color is light yellow-brown.

Point Color Patterns

Ragdolls may have solid points, lynx points, or tortie points. Ragdolls with lynx points have lightly striped coats and heavily striped points. Tortie-point Ragdolls have points with patches of black, red, and cream.

FACT: The points and color patterns of a Ragdoll darken as the cat gets older.

OTHER COLOR PATTERNS

Some Ragdolls are mitted. Like colorpoints, these cats have dark points and light-colored bodies. But a mitted Ragdoll has white mitts on its front paws. White "boots" are on its back legs and feet. A mitted Ragdoll also has a white stripe on its stomach, a white chin, and a white chest.

Van Ragdolls are mostly white. They have dark markings on their ears, tail, and the top area of their face. They also may have a couple of dark markings on their bodies.

mitted Ragdoll

FACT: Each registry has different rules about which Ragdoll colors and patterns are allowed in cat shows.

bi-color Ragdoll

Bi-color Ragdolls have dark points on their ears, tail, and the outer part of their faces. All four legs, the underbody, and the chest are white. Bi-colors have a white upside-down "V" marking on their faces. They also may have some white on their backs.

FACIAL FEATURES

A Ragdoll's head is wide and shaped like a wedge. This shape looks like an upside-down triangle. Its ears are wide at the base and rounded at the top. The ears also tip forward. All Ragdolls have blue, oval-shaped eyes.

PERSONALITY

Ragdolls are friendly cats. They seem to enjoy being around people and other animals. Although they don't crave constant attention, Ragdolls may follow people around. They seem to enjoy quietly watching the people and animals around them. Ragdolls also seem to enjoy being held.

Ragdolls are known for their intelligence. Many can be trained to play fetch or to follow other basic commands.

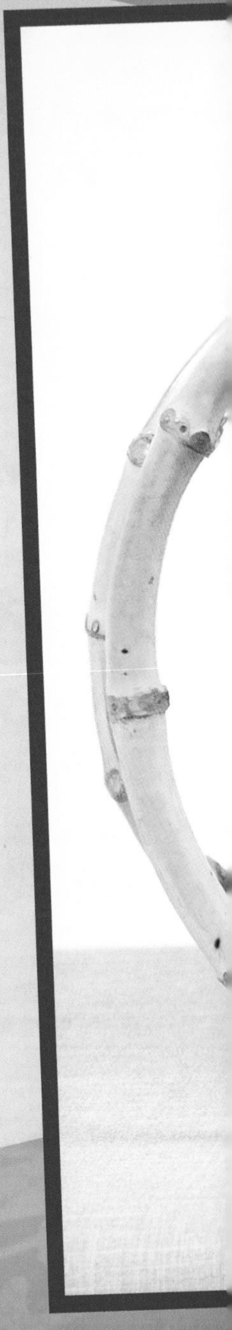

FACT: Many cats seem to enjoy jumping onto tall objects. But Ragdolls often stay on the floor instead.

Kittens have a curious nature. They may climb into bags or purses to investigate the contents.

Chapter 4

CARING FOR A RAGDOLL

Ragdolls are strong, healthy cats. With proper care, owners can have a healthy companion for many years. Ragdolls can live 15 years or more.

You can help your cat live a healthy life by keeping it inside. Cats that are allowed to roam outdoors face dangers from cars and other animals. They are also more likely to develop diseases.

FEEDING

Like all cats, Ragdolls need high-quality food. Most cat foods in supermarkets and pet stores will provide a balanced, healthy diet for your Ragdoll.

Some owners feed their cats dry food. This food usually is less expensive than other food. Dry food can help keep cats' teeth clean. It also will not spoil if it is left in a dish.

Other owners prefer to feed their cats moist, canned food. This type of food will spoil if it is left out for more than one hour.

Cats also need to drink water to stay healthy. Owners should keep their cats' bowls filled with fresh, clean water. Owners should dump and refill the water bowls each day.

FACT: Some owners feed both moist and dry food to their cats. The variety can help keep cats interested in food.

LITTER BOXES

Cat owners need to provide their cats with a **litter** box. You should clean the waste out of the box each day. Change the litter often. Cats are clean animals, and they may refuse to use a dirty litter box.

NAIL CARE

Cats need their nails trimmed every few weeks. Trimming helps reduce damage if cats scratch carpet or furniture. It also protects cats from infections caused by ingrown nails. Cats with this condition have nails that have grown into the bottom of the paw. Owners should start to trim their Ragdolls' nails when the cats are young.

litter—small bits of clay or other material used to absorb the waste of cats and other animals

Providing your cat with a scratching post can help keep your cat's nails healthy. It can also help reduce damage to furniture. Scratching posts are available at pet stores. You can also make one by attaching carpet to a short wooden post.

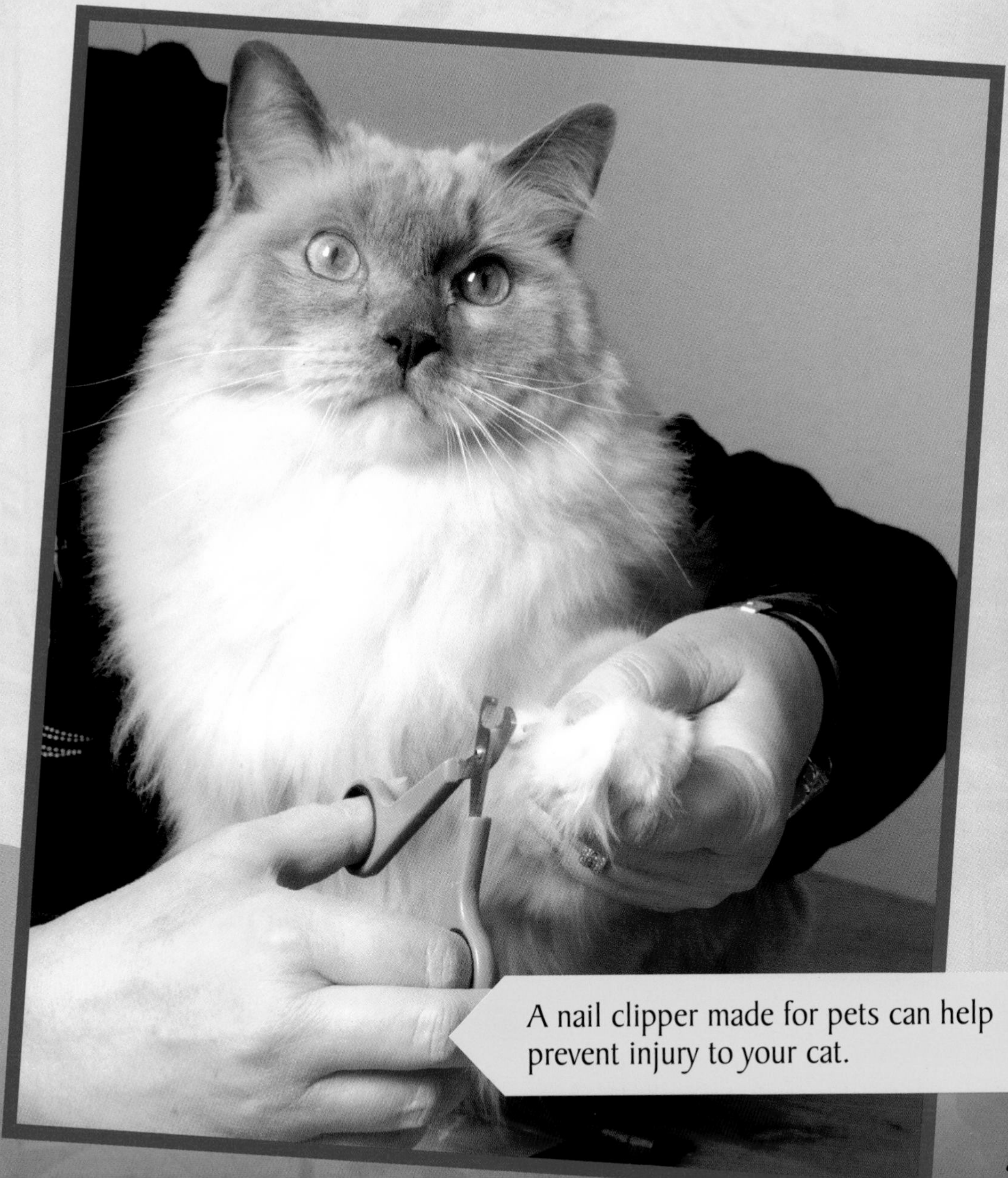

A nail clipper made for pets can help prevent injury to your cat.

Regular brushing will help keep your Ragdoll's coat smooth and shiny.

GROOMING

A Ragdoll's fur is easy to groom. It does not mat or tangle as easily as the fur of some other longhaired breeds. But you still need to brush your Ragdoll's coat once each week. You can use any type of brush, but a natural bristle brush works best. Plastic or other synthetic brushes can cause the cat's fur to stand on end from static electricity. A comb works well on thicker areas of a Ragdoll's coat.

You should brush your Ragdoll more often during spring. Ragdolls shed their winter coats at this time. Frequent brushings will help the cats get rid of loose hair.

DENTAL CARE

Cats need regular dental care to protect their teeth and gums from **plaque**. Brush your cat's teeth at least once each week. Use a special toothbrush made for cats or a soft cloth. Always use a toothpaste made for cats. Cats can become sick if they swallow toothpaste made for people.

plaque—the coating of food, saliva, and bacteria that forms on teeth and can cause tooth decay

HEALTH CARE

Ragdoll cats have few health problems. The most common problem is **hairballs**. Regular brushing is the best way to prevent hairballs. Brushing removes loose fur before the cat can swallow it.

A myth about Ragdolls says the cats have bones or muscles that have not formed correctly. Some people believe that this physical deformity is the reason Ragdolls' bodies relax when held. But Ragdolls don't have any physical deformities. No one knows why some Ragdoll cats relax their muscles when they are picked up.

Veterinarians examine cats closely at checkups for signs of health problems.

FACT: Spayed and neutered cats often have calmer personalities than cats that haven't had these surgeries.

Like all cats, Ragdolls must visit a veterinarian at least once each year. New Ragdoll owners should take their cat to a vet for a checkup as soon as possible. Vets will check the cat for signs of health problems. Cats also receive any necessary **vaccinations** at checkups.

If you don't plan to breed your Ragdoll, you should have it spayed or neutered by a vet. These surgeries keep cats from having unwanted kittens. Controlling the pet population increases the chances that pets already needing homes will be adopted. Spaying and neutering also helps keep a cat from developing certain diseases.

Owning a Ragdoll is a big job. But the job comes with many rewards. Responsible owners can expect to share many happy years with their "gentle giants."

hairball—a ball of fur that lodges in a cat's stomach

vaccination—a shot of medicine that protects animals from a disease

GLOSSARY

breed (BREED)—a certain kind of animal within an animal group; breed also means to mate and raise a certain kind of animal

colorpoint (KUHL-ur-point)—a pattern in which the ears, face, tail, and feet are darker than the base color

deformity (di-FORM-it-ee)—being twisted, bent, or disfigured

hairball (HAIR-bawl)—a ball of fur that lodges in a cat's stomach

litter (LIT-ur)—small bits of clay or other material used to absorb the waste of cats and other animals

mitted (MIT-ed)—a color pattern that includes white foot markings and white on the stomach, chin, and chest

plaque (PLAK)—the coating of food, saliva, and bacteria that forms on teeth and can cause tooth decay

proportion (pruh-POR-shuhn)—the relation of one part to another; animals have good proportion when a body part doesn't seem too large or too small when compared to another

registry (REH-juh-stree)—an organization that keeps track of the ancestry for cats of a certain breed

ruff (RUHF)—long hairs growing around an animal's neck

seal-point (SEEL-POINT)—a colorpoint pattern in which the points are very dark brown

vaccination (vak-suh-NAY-shun)—a shot of medicine that protects animals from a disease

READ MORE

Landau, Elaine. *Ragdolls are the Best!* The Best Cats Ever. Minneapolis: Lerner, 2011.

Mattern, Joanne. *Maine Coon Cats.* All About Cats. Mankato, Minn.: Capstone Press, 2011.

Rau, Dana Meachen. *Top 10 Cats for Kids.* Top Pets for Kids with American Humane. Berkeley Heights, N.J.: Enslow Elementary, 2009.

Stamper, Judith Bauer. *Ragdolls: Alien Cats.* Cat-ographies. New York: Bearport, 2011.

INTERNET SITES

FactHound offers a safe, fun way to find Internet sites related to this book. All of the sites on FactHound have been researched by our staff.

Here's all you do:

Visit *www.facthound.com*

Type in this code: 9781429668675

WWW.FACTHOUND.COM®

INDEX